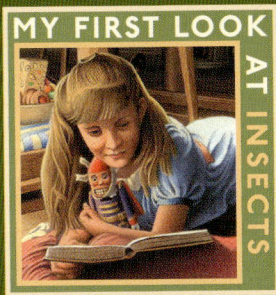

MY FIRST LOOK AT INSECTS

A SPIDER CRAWLING ON ITS WEB

Spiders

TERESA WIMMER

CREATIVE EDUCATION

Published by Creative Education

123 South Broad Street, Mankato, Minnesota 56001

Creative Education is an imprint of The Creative Company

Designed by Rita Marshall

Photographs by Getty Images (altrendo nature, Stephen Alvarez, Tony Bennett, Geoff du

Feu, Brian Kenney, Tim Laman, Peter Lilja, Buddy Mays, Sergio Pitamitz), McDonald Wildlife

(Joe McDonald)

Printed in the United States of America

Library of Congress Cataloging-in-Publication Data

Wimmer, Teresa. Spiders / by Teresa Wimmer.

p. cm. — (My first look at: insects)

Includes index.

ISBN-13 : 978-1-58341-456-9

1. Spiders—Juvenile literature. I. Title.

QL458.4.W54 2006   595.44—dc22   2005037239

First edition 9 8 7 6 5 4 3 2 1

SPIDERS

MANY SIZES, MANY HOMES

Look in a corner, and a spider might be there. Spiders live almost everywhere on Earth. They live underground, in caves, and in buildings. Some even live underwater.

There are many different kinds of spiders. Most spiders are brown, gray, or black. They come in many sizes. Some spiders are the size of a pinhead. Others are as big as a grown-up's hand.

SOME SPIDERS HAVE A BIG BODY

7

All spiders have eight legs. Sometimes a leg gets torn off. Then a new leg grows in its place. Spiders do not have bones. Instead, they have a hard skin to protect themselves from harm.

WEB WEAVING

All spiders have **spinnerets**. They use the spinnerets to make **silk**. Many spiders use their silk to spin webs. They spin them in the corners of buildings, under chairs, or in bushes.

A spider's legs are covered
with hairs. The hairs help the
spider feel and smell things.

Each spider web is a different shape. House spiders weave messy webs called "tangled webs." Grass spiders spin webs that look like cones. Other webs are shaped like bowls. Spiders make a new web every night.

Most spiders do not live in their webs. They use their webs to catch food. The webs are sticky. When an **insect** flies into the web, it cannot get out.

Spiders are careful workers.
It can take a spider three
hours to spin a web.

A Big Feast

Not all spiders use webs to catch food. Hunting spiders hide behind a tree or rock. When they see an insect, they run out to kill it. Jumping spiders sneak up on an insect. Then they jump on it.

Besides insects such as flies, spiders also eat plants. Some even eat small animals. Tarantulas are the biggest spiders. They hunt

THIS SPIDER CAUGHT AN INSECT IN ITS WEB

for food at night. They like to eat beetles, mice, and lizards.

All spiders have **fangs**. The fangs are filled with poison that kills insects. Most spiders' poison does not hurt people. But a bite from the black widow spider can kill a person.

A BLACK WIDOW SPIDER IN A TREE

Do Not Be Afraid

Many people are afraid of spiders. But spiders bite only to protect themselves or to catch food. In fact, spiders are afraid of people. Many spiders hide when a person or animal gets too close.

Spiders can even be helpful to people. Some spiders eat insects such as grasshoppers that harm plants in fields. Spiders eat

Most spiders have
eight eyes. But they
cannot see very well.

SPIDERS LOOK SCARY, BUT MOST ARE HARMLESS

mosquitoes, too. That means there are not as many mosquitoes around to bite people!

Some people keep spiders as pets. They put the spiders in a tank with dirt, tree branches, and water. They feed the spiders. Then they watch the spiders make a web or dig in the dirt!

Spiders are not truly insects.
Insects have six legs, and a
spider has eight. But most
people think of spiders as insects.

SPIDERS CAN BE FUN TO WATCH

Hands-on: Keep a Spider Web

Spider webs have many pretty patterns. You can study a spider web for a long time by keeping one.

What You Need

Talcum powder
A sheet of black construction paper
Hair spray

What You Do

1. Find an empty spider web. Make sure the spider is not in the web.
2. Sprinkle talcum powder all over the web.
3. Have a grown-up help you spray hair spray on the construction paper.
4. While the hair spray is still wet, bring the paper up against the web. The web should stick to the paper.
5. Enjoy your spider web's pretty patterns!

WATER DROPS HELP SHOW THIS WEB PATTERN

Index

Words to Know

fangs—a spider's two long, sharp teeth

insect—a small animal that has six legs

silk—a thin, soft thread that spiders make

spinnerets—small parts of a spider's body that make silk

Read More

Berger, Melvin. *Spinning Spiders*. New York: HarperCollins Publishers, 2003.

Gibbons, Gail. *Spiders*. New York: Holiday House, 1993.

Simon, Seymour. *Spiders*. New York: HarperCollins Publishers, 2003.

Explore the Web

American Humane Association: Just for Kids http://www.americanhumane.org/kids/spiders.htm

CanTeach: Spiders http://www.canteach.ca/elementary/songspoems46.html

World Kids Network: Spiders http://worldkids.net/critters/bugs/spiders.htm